The Red Beast

Helping Children on the Autism Spectrum to Cope with Angry Feelings

K.I. Al-Ghani

Illustrated by Haitham Al-Ghani

Jessica Kingsley Publishers
London and Philadelphia

First edition published in 2008 by Jessica Kingsley Publishers
This revised edition published in Great Britain in 2022
by Jessica Kingsley Publishers
An imprint of Hodder & Stoughton Ltd
An Hachette Company

1

A CIP catalogue record for this title is available from the
British Library and the Library of Congress

ISBN 978 1 83997 275 1
eISBN 978 1 83997 276 8

Printed and bound in China by Leo Paper Products Ltd.

Jessica Kingsley Publishers' policy is to use papers that are
natural, renewable and recyclable products and made
from wood grown in sustainable forests. The logging and
manufacturing processes are expected to conform to the
environmental regulations of the country of origin.

Jessica Kingsley Publishers
Carmelite House
50 Victoria Embankment
London, EC4Y 0DZ, UK

www.jkp.com

by the same author

Winston Wallaby Can't Stop Bouncing
What to do about hyperactivity
in children including those
with ADHD, SPD and ASD
K.I. Al-Ghani
Illustrated by Haitham Al-Ghani
ISBN 978 1 78592 403 3
eISBN 978 1 78450 761 9

Are You Feeling Cold, Yuki?
A Story to Help Build Interoception and
Internal Body Awareness for Children
with Special Needs, including those
with ASD, PDA, SPD, ADHD and DCD
K.I. Al-Ghani
Illustrated by Haitham Al-Ghani
ISBN 978 1 78775 692 2
eISBN 978 1 78775 691 5

The Disappointment Dragon
Learning to cope with disappointment
(for all children and dragon tamers,
including those with Asperger Syndrome)
K.I. Al-Ghani
Illustrated by Haitham Al-Ghani
ISBN 978 1 84905 432 4
eISBN 978 0 85700 780 3

The Panicosaurus
Managing Anxiety in Children Including
Those with Asperger Syndrome
K.I. Al-Ghani
Illustrated by Haitham Al-Ghani
ISBN 978 1 84905 356 3
eISBN 978 0 85700 706 3

This book is dedicated to the memory of a dear husband and devoted father, Ahmed M.I. Al-Ghani, and to Sarah Al-Ghani for her love, support and encouragement.

A word from the author

Parents of children with special needs will agree that any uncontrollable outburst of rage can often be frightening to see and extremely difficult to manage and safely support.

Behavioural Science teaches us that when a child (or adult) is angry, they simply cannot listen or be reasoned with. Adrenaline levels can soar and this makes communication almost impossible. All attempts to placate the individual may just add fuel to the fire and can often result in injury and/or destruction, followed by a huge crash in self-esteem as the anger finally abates and adrenaline levels plummet.

Over the years, I have come to believe that teaching techniques that can be used independently to control the anger is the only way to ensure a reasonable outcome when emotions get out of control.

Some children with special educational needs like Autism Spectrum Disorder (ASD), Pathological Demand Avoidance (PDA), Sensory Processing Disorders (SPD), Attention Deficit Disorders (ADD & ADHD) and Developmental Cognitive Delays (DCD) can be prone to regular outbursts of rage, since simply living through a normal day is often fraught with anxiety and frustration. The more verbal and self-aware children can take any attempt to help as a personal criticism and some may suffer from low self-esteem, especially when they see the results of their uncontrollable emotions.

By starting early and depersonalizing the anger, it is possible to enable the child to see that anger is like a "beast" inside all of us, which needs to be tamed. Taming the "beast" can be hugely satisfying and can lead to an increase in self-esteem, not a decrease. By teaching techniques to children when they are fully in control of their tempers, role playing these visualization techniques frequently, and then setting up a place to which the children can be directed when the "beast" awakens, it is possible to lessen the frequency and ferocity of anger and give control back to the children. The aftermath of this sort of intervention is always positive and the children's success in calming the Red Beast can be acknowledged at the earliest opportunity so that self-esteem is restored. This prevents the often destructive post-mortem many children are forced to live through once the incident is over. Questioning the children serves no useful purpose and, more often than not, leads to a negative real-life memory bank and the reinforcement of the very behaviour you hope to change.

I have included more tried-and-tested strategies at the end of the book that can be used to supplement the basic visualization techniques outlined in the story.

Let's imagine that...

Deep inside everyone a Red Beast lies sleeping.

When it is asleep, the Red Beast is quite small.

However, when it wakes up, it begins to grow and grow. Strangely, as it grows, its ears begin to shrink, its eyes get smaller and smaller, and yet its mouth grows

bigger **and bigger!**

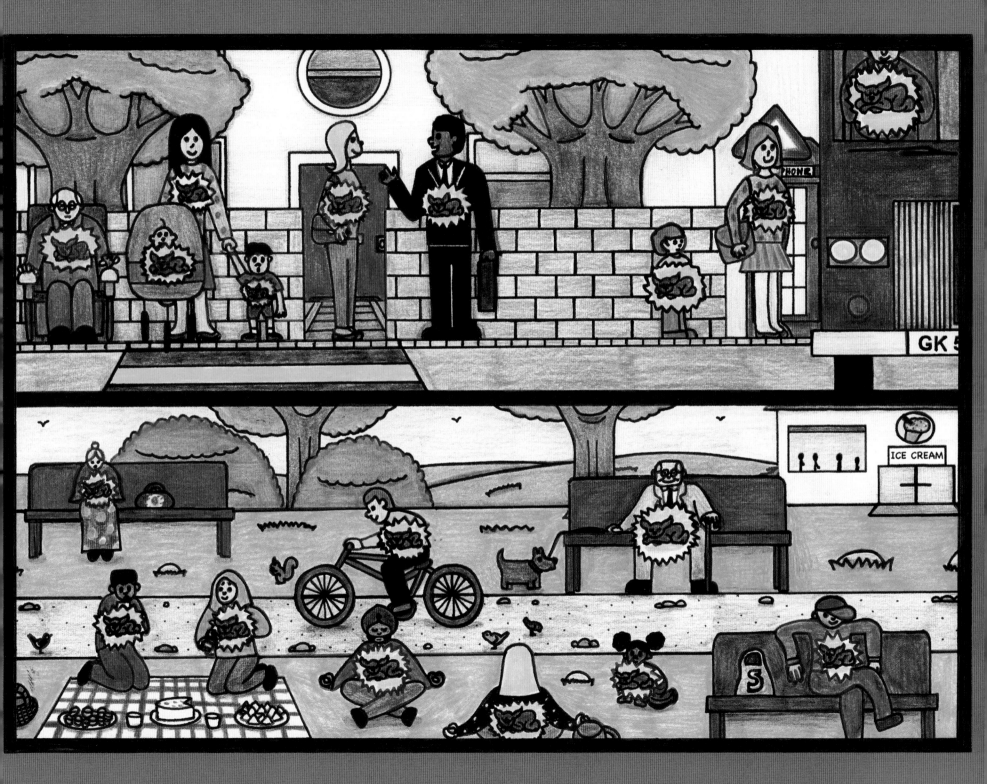

When fully awake, the Red Beast has tiny ears; it can't listen!

It has tiny eyes; it can't see very well. It has a huge mouth; it always shouts!

The Red Beast screams and calls out hurtful words like:

"I hate you!"
"Go away, leave me alone!"

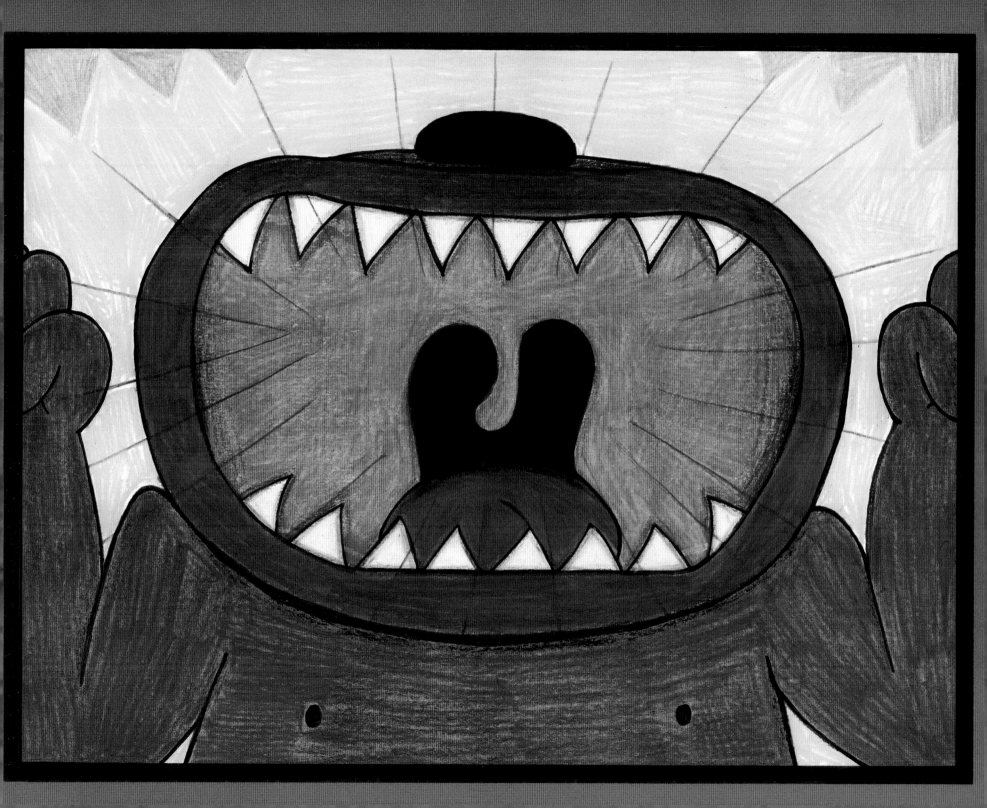

The Red Beast does hurtful things like biting, kicking, throwing, spitting and swearing!

In some people the Red Beast is very hard to wake up; it is in a deep, deep sleep.
In other people it can wake up quickly; it is only in a light sleep...

This is the story of a Red Beast that woke up...

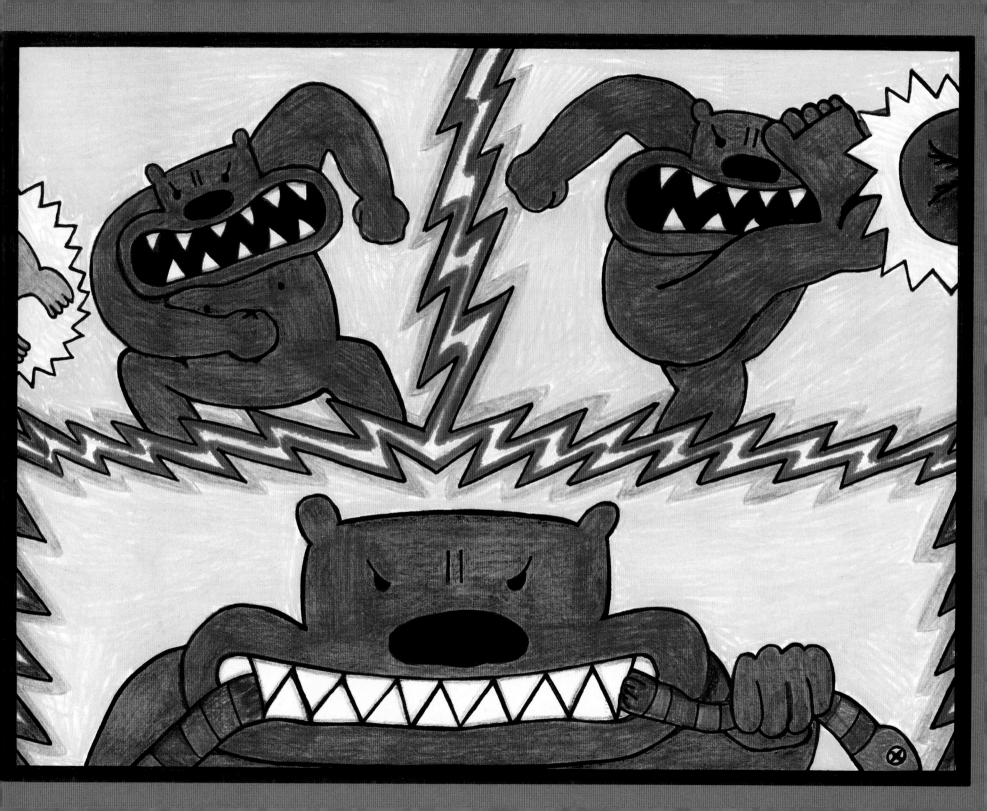

One bright morning a boy, called Danni, was in the school playground waiting for the bell to ring. Danni did not like the playground because it was noisy and this sometimes made him feel afraid.

Suddenly someone kicked a ball and it hit Danni in the stomach!

Danni was not badly hurt, but he felt very cross and he looked around angrily to see who had kicked the ball.

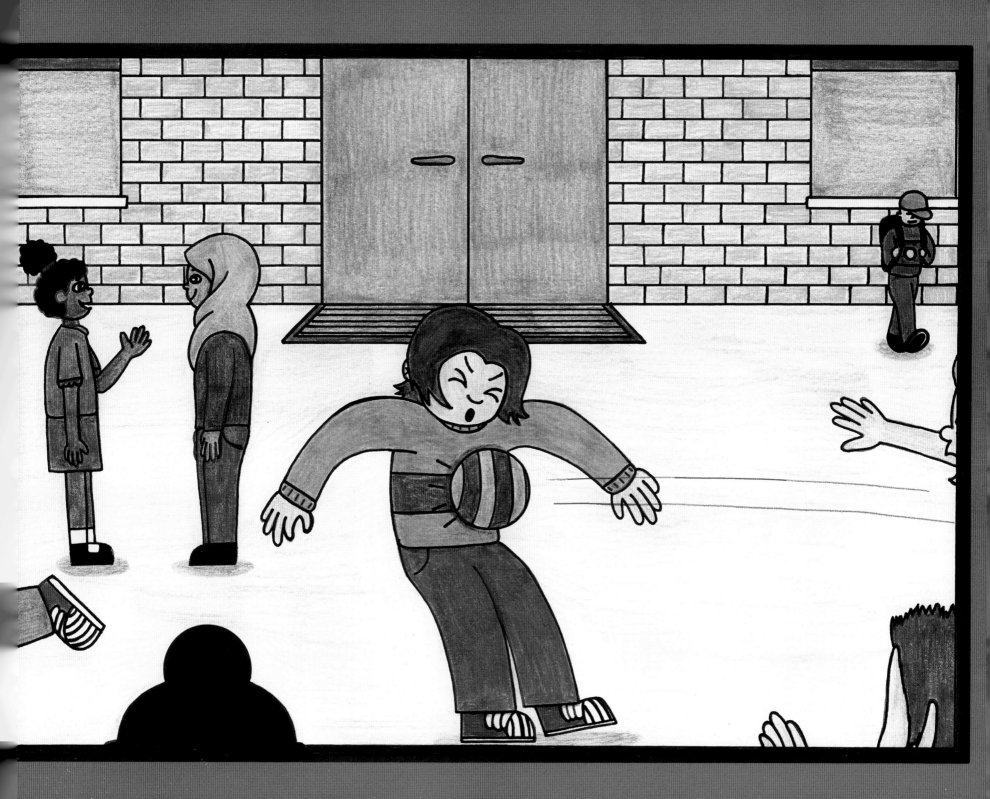

The Red Beast in Danni had woken up!

It started to grow and grow.

One of the teachers noticed that Danni was looking angry and came over to him.

"Are you all right, Danni?" asked the teacher, kindly.

But the Red Beast had tiny ears; it couldn't listen.

Charlie, the boy who had kicked the ball, ran over to Danni. "I'm really, really sorry, Danni," said Charlie sadly.

However, the Red Beast had tiny eyes and it could not see how sorry Charlie was.

The Red Beast said hurtful words and it tried to hit out at poor Charlie.

"I hate you! I'm gonna get you!"

it screamed with rage.

Charlie felt afraid and he started to cry.

More teachers came to help.

They took Danni and his Red Beast to a quiet room in the school.

The Red Beast **kicked** and **screamed**.

It spat at the teachers and shouted hurtful words.

No one looked or spoke to the beast; they just took it into the school and to the quiet room.

Danni had been in this quiet room before.

The teachers gave Danni a stress ball.

"Try to tame the Red Beast, Danni," they said kindly. "You know what to do."

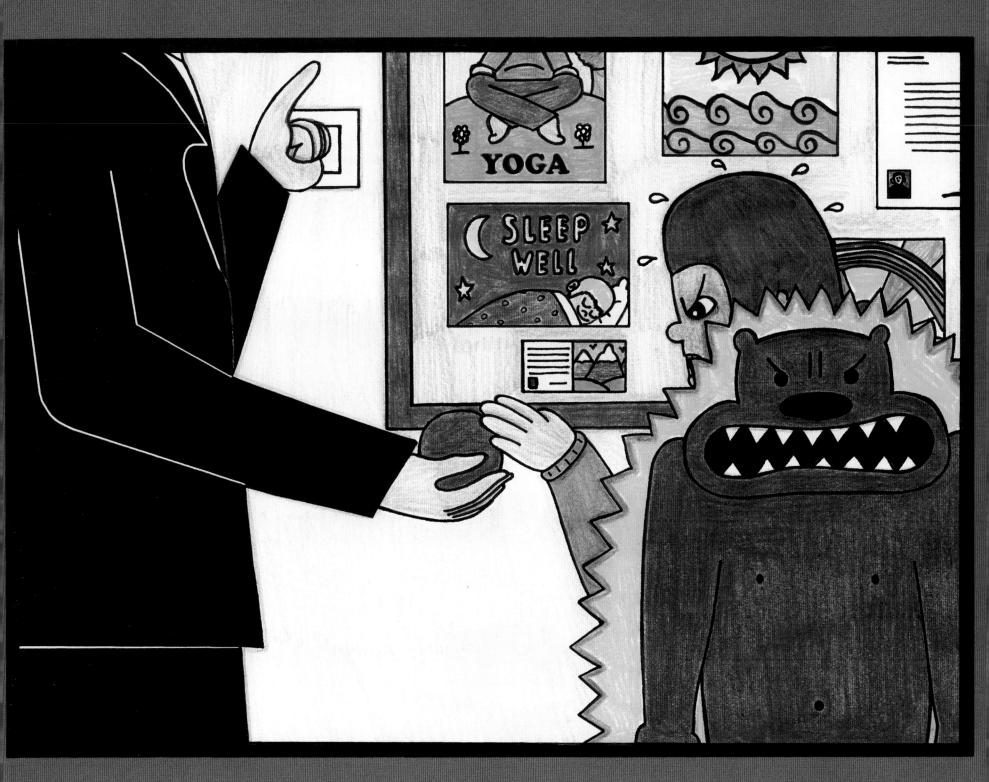

Danni took a deep breath and **squeezed** the stress ball. Then he started to count, very slowly.

"One...two...three...four...five..." he said through gritted teeth.

The Red Beast began to get smaller.

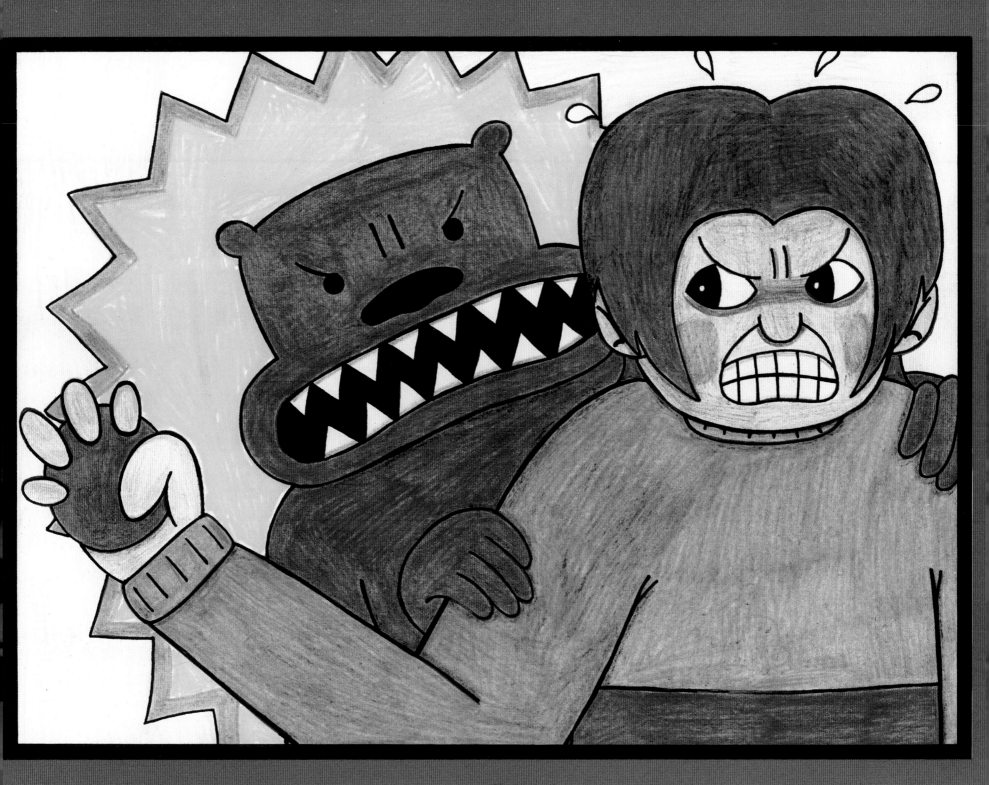

"Six...seven...eight...nine...ten..."

The Red Beast felt sleepy. Its ears and eyes grew bigger and its mouth grew smaller.

"Eleven...twelve...thirteen...fourteen...fifteen..."
counted Danni.

The Red Beast grew smaller and smaller and it felt sleepier and sleepier.

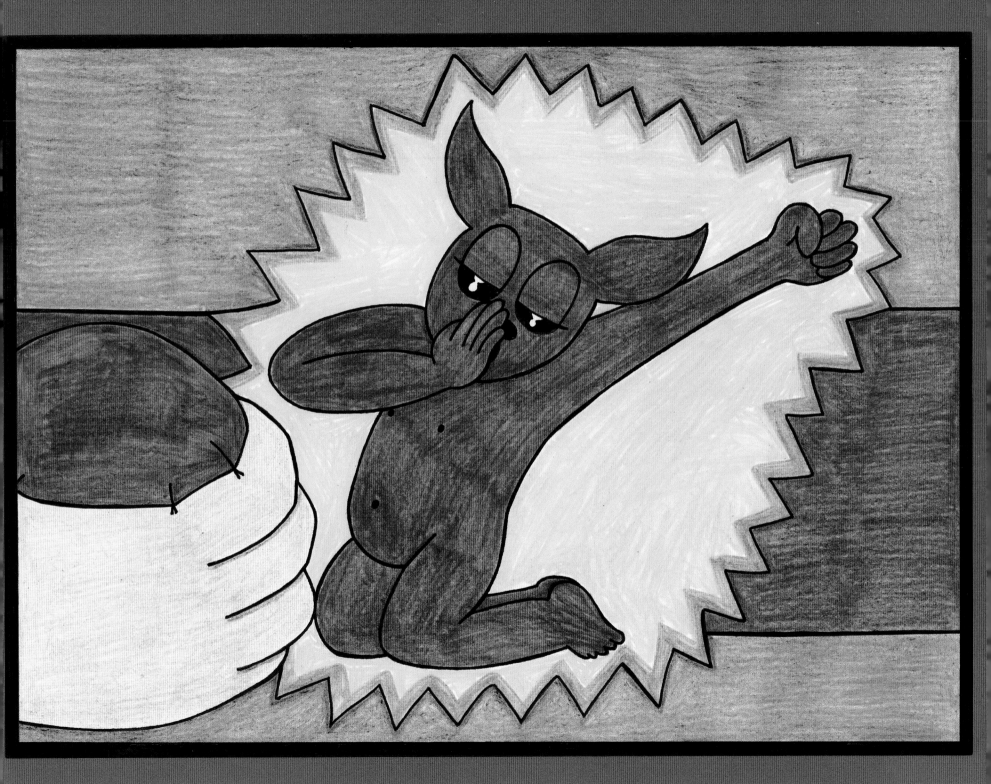

"Sixteen...seventeen...eighteen...nineteen...twenty..."
said Danni, as he slowly squeezed the stress ball.

The Red Beast began to snore.

One of the teachers looked in on Danni and gave him some cold water to drink. Danni sucked thirstily at the straw.

"Good work, Danni. Now, would you like a foot massage and some soothing music for ten minutes or a quick burst on the bubble wrap?" asked the teacher with a wink.

"Oh, bubble wrap I think," said Danni, shyly.

Danni took a sheet of green-coloured bubble wrap from the "Red Beast Box" and started popping the bubbles with relish.

After a few minutes he felt much better and was ready to go back to the classroom.

"Well done, Danni," beamed Mr Parker, his teacher. "You've tamed the Red Beast. Put ten beans in the class jar."

Danni knew that when the jar was full of beans, the whole class would get a special treat.

Danni felt tired, but very proud. He noticed Charlie looking at him from the seat near the door. Danni winked at Charlie and Charlie winked back.

Danni walked over to Charlie's table.

"I'm really sorry I got so angry with you, Charlie," said Danni sadly.

"Oh, that's okay. It wasn't you, it was that Red Beast. It's brilliant that you managed to tame him so quickly!" said Charlie, smiling.

Danni knew that taming the Red Beast wasn't easy and it would probably wake up again. However, now that he knew what to do, it would get easier and easier to put that Red Beast back to sleep.

Other strategies

- Conduct an ABC of behaviour (Antecedent, Behaviour, Consequence) to determine if you can pinpoint any flash points, so that these can be avoided.
- Use minimal language. Do not ask questions or insist on an apology. These issues are best dealt with during circle time and only when the children are quite calm and happy.
- Ensure the children know where to go and who to approach if they feel out of control.
- Remain calm and dispassionate at all times. You may need to practise this!
- Use soothing music and eye masks. (Sometimes covering the eyes briefly when children are engaged in aggressive situations, like hair pulling, can help to dispel the violence by disorientating them.)
- Provide the children with foods to eat that will replenish blood sugar levels, for example, dates or grapes, and give them plenty of iced water – to be drunk through a straw.
- Ask the children if they would enjoy a foot massage. (Often it is necessary to remove shoes in the event of kicking, so this is a good way to reintroduce the shoes.)
- Lower yourself to the children's level.
- Look at the situation during circle time, use puppets to depersonalize the event and ask the children to think up alternative solutions. You will be surprised at how the culprits often have the best ideas!
- Give the children physical jobs like shredding paper, ripping up old material, popping the bubbles on bubble wrap – I love this one!
- Put together a Red Beast Box that includes a stress ball, eye masks, bubble wrap, relaxation CDs, a scented pillow (lavender), small night lights to use if you like the room to be darkened during relaxation times, a water bottle with a straw, foods to replenish blood sugar, like dates, raisins or grapes. Perhaps the whole class could have a relaxation session at the end of each school day – transitions are often troublesome.

If all else fails, use these techniques on yourself!

For children with special needs, anger can be the default emotion they go to when they are feeling out of sorts. They could be hungry or thirsty, too hot, too cold, too tired, in pain or anxious about something. This inability to recognize internal bodily states is caused by a lack of interoception. Training children how to improve their internal body awareness can lead to better emotional regulation – for help with this see *Are You Feeling Cold, Yuki? A Story to Help Build Interoception and Internal Body Awareness for Children with Special Needs, including those with ASD, PDA, SPD, ADHD and DCD*.